-4.20

DATE DUE

DEC 1 9 2000	JUN 2 8 2003
MAR 1 9 2001	
AUG 1 4 2001	SEP 1 2 2003
AUG 1 4 2001	
SEP 9 - 2001	FEB 2 9 2004
	DEC 1 1 2004
FEB 0 9 2002	OCT 4 - 2005
	APR 1 2 2006
MAR 2 3 2002	
APR 2 3 2002	DEC 3 - 2006
DEC 1 2002	APR 1 0 2007
	AUG 0 3 2007
DEC 1 5 2002	
	MAY 1 5 2008
APR 1 9 2003	

SCIENCE PROJECTS

WEATHER

Chris Oxlade

Photography by
Chris Fairclough

RSVP®
RAINTREE
STECK-VAUGHN
PUBLISHERS
The Steck-Vaughn Company

Austin, Texas

Published by Raintree Steck-Vaughn Publishers, an imprint of Steck-Vaughn Company.

Library of Congress Cataloging-in-Publication Data
Oxlade, Chris.
Weather/ Chris Oxlade.
    p.   cm.—(Science Projects)
    Includes bibliographical references and index.
    Summary: Introduces basic concepts of weather, discussing such topics as atmospheric pressure, clouds, rain, and wind.
    ISBN 0-8172-4949-4
    1. Weather—Juvenile literature.
    2. Meteorology—Juvenile literature.
    [1. Weather. 2. Meteorology.]
    I. Fairclough, Chris, ill. II. Title. III. Series: Science projects.
    QC981.3.095   1999
    551.5—dc21   97-41171

Printed in Italy. Bound in the United States.
1 2 3 4 5 6 7 8 9 0 02 01 00 99 98

Picture acknowledgments:
The publishers would like to thank the following for permission to reproduce their pictures:
Bruce Coleman: page 9 (Johnny Johnson), 11 (George McCarthy), 12 (Staffan Widstrand), 34 (Hans Reinhard), 42 (Hans-Peter Merten);
Getty Images: page 4 (Lori Adamski Peek), 6 (Patrick Ingrand), 10 (John Warden), 14 (Daryl Balfour), 16 (Frans Lanting), 20 (Chip Porter), 24, 28 (Alastair Black), 32 (Lorne Resnick), 38 (Peter Rauter); **Oxford Scientific Films:** page 44 (Richard Packwood); **Science Photo Library:** cover (Keith Kent), page 36 (Kent Wood), 41 (NASA).

Illustrations: Stefan Chabluk
Cover: Julian Baker

CONTENTS

EARTH'S ATMOSPHERE

The weather plays an important part in all our lives. It affects many of the everyday things we do, from taking an umbrella with us when we go on a picnic to putting on sunscreen to protect our skin. For farmers, sailors, and pilots, however, a knowledge of what the weather might do is even more crucial. Gale-force winds or driving rain can ruin crops or blow a ship off course. Even more extreme weather conditions, such as hurricanes or floods, can lead to loss of homes and lives.

The earth is surrounded by a thick blanket of air, stretching far out into space. This is the atmosphere. Ninety-nine percent of all the air in the atmosphere is below an altitude (height) of 30 mi. (50 km). Eighty percent lies in the troposphere, the bottom layer of the atmosphere. This is where the weather happens.

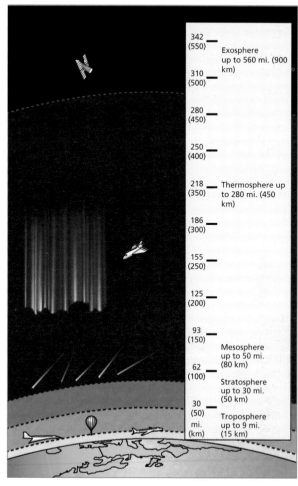

mi. (km)	
342 (550)	Exosphere up to 560 mi. (900 km)
310 (500)	
280 (450)	
250 (400)	
218 (350)	Thermosphere up to 280 mi. (450 km)
186 (300)	
155 (250)	
125 (200)	
93 (150)	Mesosphere up to 50 mi. (80 km)
62 (100)	Stratosphere up to 30 mi. (50 km)
30 (50)	Troposphere up to 9 mi. (15 km)

There is a close relationship between weather and air pressure. Air appears to weigh nothing at all, but it is heavier than you might think. In the atmosphere above the earth, the weight of the air presses downward, compressing the air below. This air pressure presses on everything, not just downward, but in all directions. A change in air pressure usually means a change in the weather.

Having fun in the snow is a feature of winter weather in many parts of the world.

AIR HAS WEIGHT

MATERIALS
- 2 ft. (60 cm) of dowel or thin garden cane
- 2 balloons
- string
- tape
- a straight pin
- a ruler
- a pencil
- scissors

1. Make a pencil mark on the dowel .3 in. (1 cm) from either end. Blow up two balloons as far as they will go and tie them to the ends of the dowel where the marks are. Cut a piece of tape about 2 in. (5 cm) long and stick it firmly onto one of the balloons.

2. Tie one end of a length of string to the middle of the dowel. Use the string to hang the dowel in mid-air (you could attach it to the top of a door frame with tape).

3. Move the knot in the middle of the dowel to the left or right until the dowel hangs exactly level.

4. With a pin, carefully make three or four holes in the tape on one of the balloons. Hold the balloons and dowel to stop them from swinging, then let go.

5. After a few minutes all the air will have escaped from the punctured balloon. The cane is no longer horizontal. Which end is higher? Can you explain why this happens?

UNDER PRESSURE

MATERIALS
- an empty plastic bottle

Remove the top from the plastic bottle and wash the neck with water. Put your mouth over the neck and suck gently. What have you done to the air pressure inside the bottle? What does the higher air pressure outside the bottle do to the shape of the bottle?

5

ATMOSPHERIC PRESSURE

The pressure exerted by the air in the atmosphere is called air pressure or atmospheric pressure. It is greatest at the bottom of the atmosphere because the air is thickest there. At sea level, atmospheric pressure presses down with one kilogram's worth of push for every square centimeter (14 lbs per sq. in.) of our skin. It exerts the same pressure on our surroundings, too.

Atmospheric pressure does not always stay the same. By monitoring changes in atmospheric pressure, we can find out what sort of weather to expect.

Falling pressure means that wet and often windy weather is on the way. Rising pressure means fine weather is on the way. Atmospheric pressure is measured with an instrument called a barometer. There are two main types of barometers—the liquid column barometer and the aneroid barometer.

In a liquid column barometer, atmospheric pressure outside supports the liquid inside a narrow tube. The top of the tube is sealed so that no air can get in. As the atmospheric pressure outside changes, the level of the top of the column rises or falls.

Inside an aneroid barometer is a small metal box with some of the air removed from it. As atmospheric pressure goes up or down, the box gets slightly smaller or bigger, causing a needle to move around a scale.

Meteorologists measure pressure in millibars (mb). Normally, atmospheric pressure is between 950 and 1,050 millibars.

An area of high pressure can bring fine, sunny weather with small, puffy clouds.

LIQUID COLUMNS

1. Stand the dowel next to the bottle.

2. Use tape to attach the dowel to the bottle and hold it.

3. Put one end of the plastic tubing into the bottle and attach the tubing along the dowel with pieces of tape.

4. Pour water into the bottle until the end of the tubing is an inch or two (a few cm) below the surface. Add several drops of food coloring to make the water easy to see.

5. Mark the dowel 4 in. (10 cm) from the top.

6. Suck the top of the tubing so that water rises up it. When the water reaches the 4-in. (10-cm) mark, squeeze the tubing to keep the water level from falling. Push some clay into the end of the tubing, fold the tubing over, and attach a crocodile clip. Tape it down, still ensuring that the water level does not drop. This should make an airtight seal.

7. Check the level of the water every day. Has it risen or fallen? What does this tell you about changes in atmospheric pressure?

UNDER THE SUN

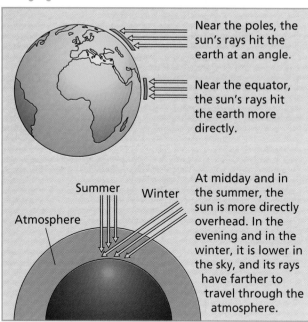

Near the poles, the sun's rays hit the earth at an angle.

Near the equator, the sun's rays hit the earth more directly.

At midday and in the summer, the sun is more directly overhead. In the evening and in the winter, it is lower in the sky, and its rays have farther to travel through the atmosphere.

Weather is governed by the position of the sun and the angle at which its rays hit the earth.

The sun provides all the energy needed to make the weather happen. This energy travels to the earth as heat rays, which pass through the atmosphere and hit the ground. These rays heat the ground, which in turn heats the air above it.

Have you noticed that the sun feels hotter in the middle of the day than it does in the early morning or evening? That is because the sun's rays have to travel different distances through the atmosphere at different times of the day. When the sun is directly overhead, at midday, the rays have the shortest distance to travel through the atmosphere.

LIGHT AND DARK

1. Cut two pieces of cardboard about 8 in. (20 cm) square. Cut a piece of white poster board the same size and attach it with rubber bands to one of the pieces of thick cardboard. Cover the other piece the same way, using the black poster board.

2. Put the box on the ground in full sunlight with one side pointing toward the sun. Rest the two pieces of cardboard against it, with the white and black sides facing the sun, so that the sun's rays hit them at right angles (90 degrees).

3. After fifteen minutes, feel the pieces of poster board. Which is warmer? Try measuring the temperature difference between the two by sliding a thermometer between the thick cardboard and the poster board. Which color is best at absorbing the sun's heat?

MATERIALS

- a sheet of thick stiff cardboard
- a large cardboard box
- a sheet of thin white poster board
- a sheet of thin black poster board
- thin rubber bands
- a thermometer
- a ruler
- a pencil
- scissors

When the sun is low in the sky, in the morning or evening, the rays hit the atmosphere at an angle and have farther to travel before they hit the ground. This makes them weaker. When the rays hit the ground at a low angle, they are spread out over a greater area. This reduces their heating effect on the ground. When the sun is high in the sky, its rays strike the ground at right angles and the heat is much more intense. Usually, the sun is highest in the sky in the summer and at midday.

At the North Pole, the sun's rays strike the ground at a low angle.

At the earth's poles, the sun never rises high in the sky. In addition, the ice and snow at the poles reflect the rays away from the ground. These two factors combine to keep the poles very cold all year round. The situation is different near the equator. Here the sun rises high in the sky every day, making the ground very hot during the daytime.

4. Replace the white poster board with another piece of black poster board. Place this in the sun's rays so that the rays hit it at 45 degrees instead of at right angles.

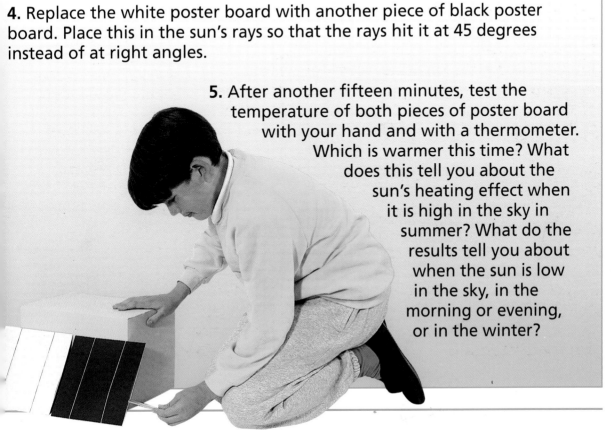

5. After another fifteen minutes, test the temperature of both pieces of poster board with your hand and with a thermometer. Which is warmer this time? What does this tell you about the sun's heating effect when it is high in the sky in summer? What do the results tell you about when the sun is low in the sky, in the morning or evening, or in the winter?

THE SEASONS

In many parts of the world, the weather is generally wet and cold for six months of the year and generally drier and hotter for the other six months. These changes in weather are called the seasons. Seasons are caused by changes in temperature, which, in turn, are caused by the relationship between the earth and the sun. While the earth moves in an orbit around the sun, it tilts on its axis (this is the imaginary line running through the earth from the North to the South pole), always leaning in the same direction.

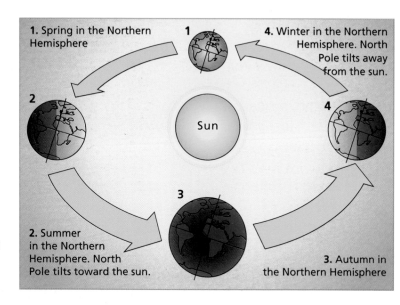

1. Spring in the Northern Hemisphere

4. Winter in the Northern Hemisphere. North Pole tilts away from the sun.

Sun

2. Summer in the Northern Hemisphere. North Pole tilts toward the sun.

3. Autumn in the Northern Hemisphere

The earth's tilted orbit around the sun means that when it is winter in the Northern Hemisphere, it is summer in the Southern Hemisphere, and vice versa.

When the earth is on one side of the sun, the North Pole is tilted away from the sun. The sun's rays hit the Southern Hemisphere more directly than the Northern Hemisphere. This makes the Southern Hemisphere hotter, so it has summer. Meanwhile, the Northern Hemisphere has winter. Six months later, the earth has moved around its orbit to the other side of the sun. Now the South Pole is tilted away from the sun; so it is summer in the Northern Hemisphere and winter in the Southern Hemisphere.

Many animals and plants adapt their lifestyles to the changing seasons. In the autumn, birds migrate to warmer climates where they spend the winter.

The migration of these cranes indicates a change in the seasons.

Other animals, such as bears, hibernate to save energy when food is scarce. Deciduous trees save energy, too, by losing their leaves in the autumn and shutting down for the winter.

This hibernating mouse has stocked up with food before falling asleep for the winter.

SPINS AND ORBITS

MATERIALS
- a flashlight
- a globe
- a ruler
- a pencil
- a box

1. In a darkened room, place the flashlight on top of the box so that its bulb is level with the middle of the globe. The flashlight represents the sun. Make sure that it shines at the globe from a distance of from 12–16 in. (30–40 cm). The globe's axis should be leaning away from the flashlight.

2. Before investigating the seasons, slowly turn the globe. This represents the day passing by. Can you see how parts of the globe are first in sunlight and then in shadow? Which parts of the earth receive the most sunshine? What season is it in the Northern Hemisphere?

3. Now move the globe along its orbit around the sun (you'll need to swing the flashlight around, too). Keep the axis pointing in the same direction all the time. Can you see how the seasons change?

AIR ON THE MOVE

A gliding condor hitches a free ride on a thermal, a pocket of rising air.

When air gets warmer, it expands (takes up more space). This has two effects: first, it makes the warmed air thinner, or less dense (and because of this, it floats upward in the denser air around it); second, the pressure of the warm air falls. So what happens when air gets cooler? It does the opposite: it contracts (takes up less space), becomes thicker (or denser), and sinks toward the ground. The pressure of the cool air increases.

On a sunny day, the ground gets very hot and heats the air above it. The warm air becomes less dense and floats upward, creating a column of

BALLOON TRICKS

MATERIALS
- 2 balloons
- tape
- a plastic bottle
- a bowl of hot water

1. Blow up a balloon and tie a knot in the neck. Carefully stick a strip of tape around the middle. Put the balloon in a freezer.

2. After a few minutes, take the balloon out and examine it. Has the tape wrinkled? What has happened to the air in the balloon?

3. Stretch the neck of another balloon over the mouth of a plastic bottle. Stand the bottle in a bowl of hot water for a few seconds. Hold the bottle steady or it will fall over. Why do you think the balloon begins to inflate?

rising air, called a thermal. Birds of prey and glider pilots use thermals to help them stay in the air.

On a hot day at the beach, you might notice a light wind blowing inland from the sea. This is called a sea breeze. Sea breezes occur because warm air above the land rises, and cooler air from the sea rushes in to replace it. At night, the land cools down more quickly than the sea. Cold air over the land pushes out to sea, causing a land breeze.

Huge areas of rising and falling air cause areas of high pressure, called anticyclones, or "highs," and areas of low pressure, called depressions, or "lows," in the atmosphere. Air flowing from highs to lows creates the world's winds.

AIR SPINNER

1. Cut a thin cross-shape from the cardboard, wide enough to sit on top of the mug. Unfold a paper clip to make an L-shaped piece of wire. Tape this to the cross so that one end of the wire sticks up from the middle of the cross. Tape a pin to the top of the paper clip with its pointed end up.

2. Fold the strip of paper in half at an angle to make an L shape. Unfold it partway and you will have a propeller shape.

3. Fill the mug with warm water. Put the cross on top and balance the propeller on the pin. Stand back and watch. The propeller spins slowly around. Can you determine why?

MATERIALS
- a $^3/_4$ in. x 4 in. (2 cm x 10 cm) strip of paper
- thick cardboard
- a mug of warm water
- a paper clip
- a straight pin
- tape
- scissors

HOT AND COLD

Changes of temperature have a great effect on our lives. Warm clothes and central heating help us cope with the cold of winter. In the summer, heat from the sun warms our bodies. But we must be careful in the sun. We need to drink plenty of water to keep cool and keep ourselves from

Mount Kilimanjaro in Kenya always has snow at the top, even though it is in one of the hottest parts of the world.

SUN AND SHADE TEMPERATURES

1. On a sunny day, go outside with a thermometer and a notepad and pen. Hang the thermometer in a shady place, out of the sunshine. Wait for the thermometer reading to settle, then write it down.

2. Now move the thermometer into the sunshine. Wait a few minutes and read it again. What has happened to the reading?

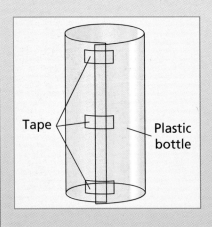

Tape — Plastic bottle

3. In order to take an accurate air temperature reading, you need to make a thermometer housing. To do this, first cut the top and bottom off the plastic bottle, to leave a tube. Keep the top part for later. Cut the tube lengthwise, and fold one side around the other to make a smaller tube. Use tape to keep it from unfolding.

MATERIALS

- a thermometer
- string
- a large plastic bottle
- aluminum foil
- a 3 ft. (1 m) piece of thick garden stake
- short pieces of dowel or thin cane
- tape
- scissors
- a notepad and pen

becoming dehydrated. Ultraviolet rays from the sun cause burning, so when you go out on a sunny day you should protect bare skin with sunscreen.

Have you noticed that it feels warm in the sunshine but much cooler in the shade? That is because the sun's rays have a greater heating effect on your skin than on the air around you. To get an accurate reading of air temperature, meteorologists always measure temperature in the shade. There are two common temperature scales—degrees Fahrenheit (°F) and degrees Celsius (°C). Temperature is measured with a thermometer. Most thermometers are liquid thermometers; these have a bulb full of colored liquid that expands when the temperature rises. When it expands, the liquid rises in a narrow tube next to the given scale.

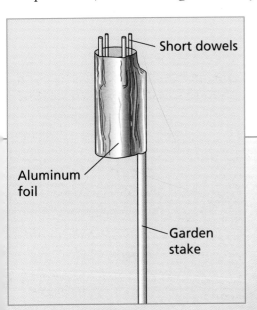

Short dowels

Aluminum foil

Garden stake

4. Tape the tube to the top of the stake. Tape four short pieces of dowel to the top of the tube. These will support the lid. Now wrap the tube in aluminum foil.

5. Tie the thermometer to a short piece of string. Lower it through the neck of the bottle and screw the bottle top on, to jam the string in place. Now cover the top with aluminum foil.

6. Go outside and push the stake into the soil. Put the lid on the tube so that the thermometer hangs inside. After a few minutes, lift off the lid and read the thermometer. It should give you an accurate air temperature. Do you know what the aluminum foil is for and why the top and bottom of the tube are open to the air?

WATER IN THE AIR

Even when it is not raining, there is water in the air around you. You cannot see it because this water is in the form of a gas, called water vapor. Water gets into the air because molecules (very tiny, invisible particles) of water escape from the surfaces of oceans, lakes, and rivers as they are heated by the sun. This process is called evaporation.

The amount of water vapor in the air is called humidity. When the air contains only a small amount of water vapor, humidity is said to be low. High humidity means that a large amount of water vapor is in the air. In high humidity, the air feels muggy and sticky. Humidity is measured with a device called a hygrometer.

The air can hold only a certain amount of water vapor before it becomes saturated and evaporation stops. Cold air cannot hold as much water vapor as warm air. This means that when warm, humid air cools down, the cooler air cannot hold all the water vapor in it.

In this steamy rain forest in Brazil, the high humidity is visible as mist.

Some of the water vapor turns back into liquid water. This is called condensation, and gives rise to effects like clouds, fog, mist, and dew.

EVAPORATION

1. Fill both saucers with water. Put them outside in a shady place next to each other. Cover one with the plastic container.

2. Keep checking the pools of water. Which one dries up first? Can you think why this happens?

MATERIALS
- two saucers
- a plastic container to fit over saucer

A PAPER STRIP HYGROMETER

1. Hook a thin rubber band onto a paper clip and tape the paper clip to one end of the strip of paper. Hook another paper clip onto the rubber band.

2. Tape the second paper clip firmly to one end of the yardstick. Pull the other end of the paper strip to stretch the rubber band slightly and then tape it at the other end of the yardstick.

MATERIALS
- a yardstick or 3-ft. (1-m) plank of wood
- 1 in. x 35 in. (2.5 cm x 90 cm) strip of paper
- a thin rubber band
- paper clips
- a cork
- a drinking straw
- scissors
- tape

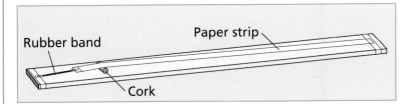

Rubber band · Paper strip · Cork

3. Tape a cork to the yardstick under the paper strip near the rubber band.

4. Unfold a paper clip to make an L shape. Cut a 1-in. (2.5 cm) piece of tape and wrap it around one part of the L with the sticky side facing out. Attach a drinking straw to the other part of the L.

5. Place the part of the L wrapped in tape between the cork and the paper strip so that the straw points upward.

6. Test the hygrometer by breathing lightly on the paper strip to make it slightly damp. (Your breath contains a small amount of water vapor.) What happens to the straw? What must have happened to the paper strip?

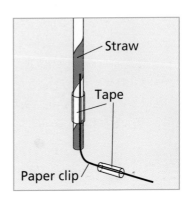

Straw · Tape · Paper clip

What happens as the paper dries out again?

CLOUDS

Clouds form in many shapes and sizes, and they change and form again throughout the day. They are the messengers of the weather, giving a good indication of what is to come.

Clouds are made of tiny droplets of water or tiny ice crystals. The water droplets and ice crystals are produced when warm, humid air cools down and some of the water vapor in it condenses, or freezes. On hot, sunny days, clouds form when warm air heated by the ground floats upward and cools. Clouds also form above mountains, as air flows up the mountainsides and cools.

Clouds are named after their shape and their position in the sky. There are three main types—cirrus (curls), stratus (layers), and cumulus (heaps). Cirrus clouds form very high in the sky and are made of ice crystals. They are often a sign of bad weather to come. Cumulus clouds look like fluffy balls of cotton; they usually bring good weather. Stratus clouds are low, gray clouds that blanket the sky and often bring drizzly rain. The largest clouds are cumulonimbus clouds; they often herald heavy rain and thunderstorms.

DID YOU KNOW?

Cumulonimbus clouds can tower more than 9 mi. (15 km) up into the sky—higher than jet airliners fly. A large cloud may contain enough water to fill 250 swimming pools.

Cloud types

Cirrus

Cumulonimbus

Cumulus

Stratus

Feet (Meters)
39,370 (12,000)
36,089 (11,000)
32,808 (10,000)
29,528 (9,000)
26,247 (8,000)
22,966 (7,000)
19,685 (6,000)
16,404 (5,000)
13,123 (4,000)
9,843 (3,000)
6,562 (2,000)
3,281 (1,000)

WATCHING WATER VAPOR

Boil a tea kettle of water. As the water begins to boil, look at the spout from the side. Can you see an almost clear gas shooting out? This is almost pure water vapor. It quickly cools and condenses into tiny droplets, which make up the steam that you can see.

A CLOUD MAKER

MATERIALS

● a large plastic bottle
● a small metal pan
● ice cubes
● a sheet of dark cardboard
● scissors

1. Carefully cut the top off the plastic bottle. Pour warm water into the bottle until it is about 2 in. (5 cm) deep. Swirl the water up the sides of the bottle a few times to warm it. This will help to keep condensation from appearing on the sides.

2. Fill a metal pan with ice cubes. Carefully balance the pan on top of the bottle. Look into the bottle. Can you see thin wisps of swirling cloud?

3. If you can't see the clouds, remove the pan, swirl the water around, and try again. Try putting the container on a windowsill so that light shines behind it, or put a piece of dark cardboard behind it. This will help you see the clouds more clearly. Can you determine how the "clouds" form?

CLOUD WATCHING

On a day with broken cloud cover, study the tops of the clouds. You could use binoculars for this.

Can you see the clouds changing shape as the air and water droplets swirl around? This swirling is easiest to see at the tops of the clouds.

RAIN

Although they look different, gloomy rain clouds and fluffy "fair weather" clouds are created the same way. So why does one produce rain and the other not? The water droplets that make up a cloud are so minute that they float in the air. To make rain, the droplets have to join to make drops heavy enough to fall.

In fluffy clouds, only a small amount of water has condensed, so the droplets or crystals lie too far apart to join and make a larger drop. When the air cools further, more droplets are made and these join to make rain. These larger droplets also give rain clouds a gray appearance.

In warm, tropical places, the water droplets join and fall as rain. In other, cooler places, the droplets freeze into ice crystals as they form in the clouds. As the air cools further, water condenses onto these ice crystals, which grow bigger until they fall. If the temperature of the air nearer the ground is above freezing, the crystals melt to make raindrops.

A cumulonimbus cloud dropping its load of rain over coastal hills. In general, coastal areas have higher rainfall than inland regions.

MEASURING RAIN

1. Cut the top off the plastic bottle just below the point at which it begins to get narrow. The bottom part of the bottle makes a simple rain collector.

2. To measure the amount of rain that has fallen, you need to make a scale on the side of the bottle. Stick a strip of poster board down the outside of the bottle. Rainfall is measured in inches (mm). Measure 1/2 in. (13 mm) from the bottom of the bottle and make a mark on the poster board. If the rainwater comes to that level, it means half an inch (13 mm) of rain has fallen. Mark the poster board in half inches (13 mm) up to 4 1/2 in. (117 mm). Cover the poster board with a layer of tape to protect it from the rain.

3. Take the cap off the top of the bottle and insert the top piece upside down into your rain collector. This will keep the collected rainwater from evaporating and giving you a false reading.

4. Put your rain collector outside in an open place, away from buildings and trees. Measure the water inside at the same time each day for a month to find out how much rain has fallen. Write down the results and use them to make a bar graph to show the amount of rain that has fallen in your area in a month.

MATERIALS

- a plastic bottle with a flat bottom
- a sheet of poster board
- a ruler
- felt-tip pens
- scissors
- tape
- graph paper

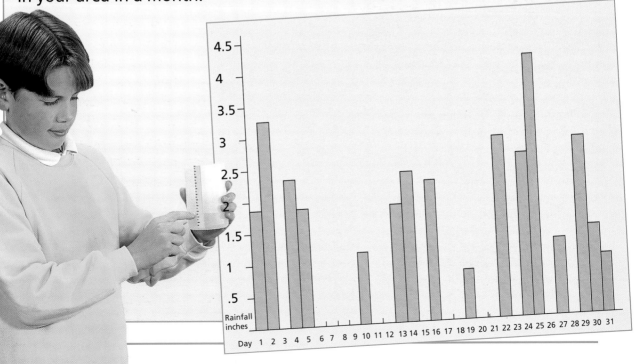

THE WATER CYCLE

The earth's water is always on the move. You can see it moving when it falls from the sky as rain, and as it flows in rivers and streams, but these movements are just a small part of the water's journey. In fact, water travels in a huge loop, called the water cycle.

At the start of the cycle, water evaporates from the seas as they are heated by the sun's rays. This water vapor is carried along in the air, and much of it forms clouds. Some clouds drop rain into the sea, while others move over the land. Additional clouds form from water that has evaporated from the soil and from ponds, lakes, and rivers. Rain falling onto the land soaks into the ground or flows into streams and rivers. The water cycle is completed when the rivers carry this water back to the sea.

Animals (including humans) and plants rely on the water cycle to get the water they need to live. Animals drink water. They also obtain it from the plants and seeds they eat. Plants take in water from the soil through their spreading systems of roots and use this water to make food.

All living things need water to survive. They rely on the water cycle (below) for every drop of water on Earth.

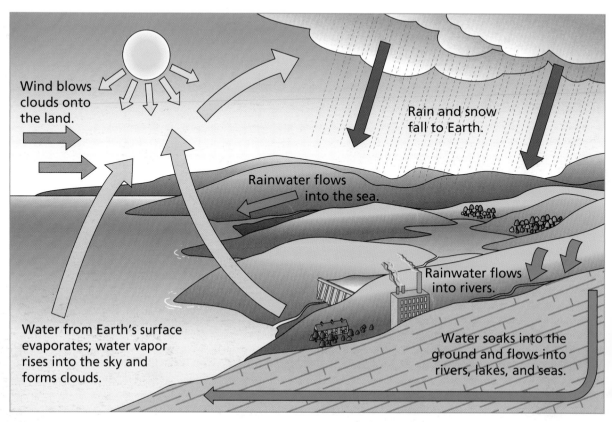

Wind blows clouds onto the land.

Rain and snow fall to Earth.

Rainwater flows into the sea.

Rainwater flows into rivers.

Water from Earth's surface evaporates; water vapor rises into the sky and forms clouds.

Water soaks into the ground and flows into rivers, lakes, and seas.

A WATER CYCLE MODEL

1. Cut a piece of blue cardboard to cover the top of the aquarium. Cut a hole about 4 in. (10 cm) square near one end of the cardboard. Cover the hole with aluminum foil so that the foil dips slightly into the hole. Secure the foil with tape.

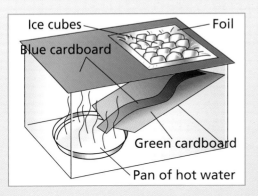

Ice cubes — Foil

Blue cardboard

Green cardboard

Pan of hot water

MATERIALS

- a clear plastic container, such as an aquarium
- a small metal pan
- aluminum foil
- plastic wrap
- tape
- ice cubes
- green cardboard
- blue cardboard
- scissors
- a ruler
- hot water

2. Put the pan in one end of the aquarium. This will be the sea.

3. Now you need to make a valley that starts at the other end of the aquarium and slopes down to the sea. Make a river using blue cardboard and stick it down the middle of the green cardboard. Cover the cardboard in plastic wrap and bend it to form a river valley.

4. Pour hot water into the pan. Position the green cardboard in the aquarium so that the river slopes down into the pan.

5. Put the lid on the aquarium with the hole positioned over the top of the valley. Carefully place the ice cubes on the aluminum foil. Watch to see what happens. Can you see water evaporating from the "sea" and condensing as "clouds" on the cold foil? What happens to the water when enough has condensed on the foil? How long does it take for the first drop of water to make its way back to the sea?

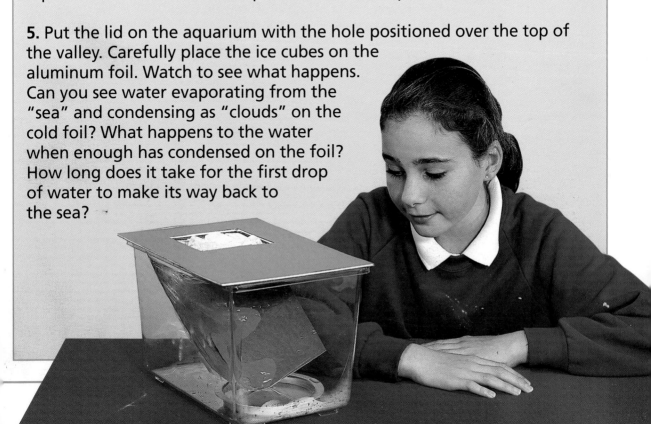

HIGHS AND LOWS

If air is warm, it rises. Where huge masses of warm air rise into the atmosphere, an area of low pressure, called a low or depression, is formed. When the rising air cools, it falls. This creates an area of high pressure, called a high or anticyclone. Near the earth's surface, air moves from areas of high pressure to areas of low pressure. This vast, swirling movement of air creates the world's winds.

This satellite photo shows a cyclonic storm system.

WEATHER MAPS

1. Find a weather map in today's newspaper. It must be a map called a synoptic chart rather than a simple weather forecast with cloud and sun symbols on it.

MATERIALS
- newspapers
- a compass
- glue
- a large sheet of cardboard

2. Look at the weather map carefully. Can you see areas marked by concentric rings of lines? They indicate areas of high or low pressure. Do they have HIGH or LOW written in them?

3. Is there a high or low near you? Look outside. From what you know about the conditions associated with high and low pressure, does the weather seem to match the chart?

4. The rings and lines on your weather chart are called isobars. These link places of equal atmospheric pressure. They are similar to contour lines on a map, which link places of equal height. Does your map have the pressure in millibars written on the isobars?

Winds do not blow in straight lines. Because the earth is spinning, the air is swung sideways as it flows, making curving winds. These winds spiral into depressions and spiral out of anticyclones. In the Northern Hemisphere, air always spins counterclockwise around a depression and clockwise around an anticyclone. The directions of spin are reversed in the Southern Hemisphere.

Anticyclones and depressions bring very different types of weather. Anticyclones usually create calm, dry weather. In the summer, they bring warm temperatures and in the winter, cold temperatures, often accompanied by frost and fog. Depressions usually create wet and windy weather. In the winter, they bring mild temperatures but strong winds and rain; in the summer, they bring cool temperatures, gray skies, and rain.

5. Cut out weather charts for a week and stick them onto a large piece of cardboard. At the end of the week you can look back at the charts and see how things have changed.

Here's a useful weather rule. Stand outside with a compass so that the wind hits you directly on your back. If you are in the Northern Hemisphere, the atmospheric pressure will go down to your left and up to your right. Things are reversed for the Southern Hemisphere. Use a compass to find the direction in which you are facing. Do your observations match today's weather chart?

WEATHER FRONTS

As the winds blow, they move great masses of air around the world. Air masses can be warm or cold or moist or dry. When two air masses collide, a weather front is formed.

There are three types of weather fronts—warm fronts, cold fronts, and occluded fronts. A warm front happens when a mass of warm air rises over a mass of cold air. A cold front happens when a mass of cold air slides underneath a mass of warm air. An occluded front is formed when a cold front catches up with a warm front.

At warm fronts and cold fronts, warm air rises and cools, creating clouds and rain. As a warm front passes by, expect several hours of steady, light rain from gray stratus clouds. Afterward, the mass of warm air brings higher temperatures. A cold front brings short, heavy downpours from huge cumulonimbus clouds. When the front has passed by, the weather becomes cold and clear.

All depressions have a warm front and cold front, which gradually merge to make an occluded front. The weather gets wetter and windier as the fronts pass by.

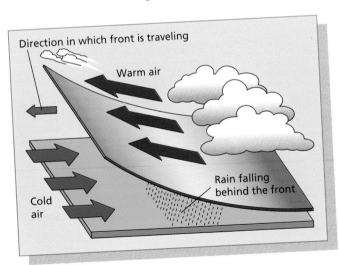

When two large air masses meet, the warm air rises gradually over the cooler air. This is a warm front.

A cold front (above) occurs when cold air pushes underneath warm air.

On weather maps, fronts are illustrated with different symbols (right).

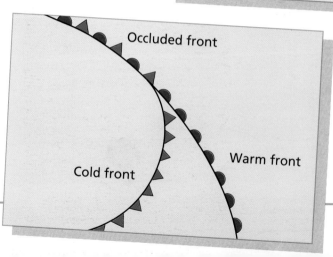

WATER WEATHER FRONTS

1. Ask an adult to cut a piece of plastic sheet into a shape that will slot into your container to divide it in two.

2. Hold the shape in place and press thin sausages of modeling clay onto the container around the edge of the sheet. Do this on both sides of the sheet to make a waterproof seal. Check that the sheet will slide up and out of the container, leaving the modeling clay in place. If the sheet is sticking to the clay, try wiggling it back and forth a little to widen the groove in the modeling clay.

3. Fill one mug with warm water and the other with cold water. Add drops of food coloring to the warm water. Pour the warm water down one side of the sheet into the container, and the cold water down the other side. Pour both in at the same time.

4. Let the water settle for a few seconds. Look into the container from the side and carefully but quickly slide out the sheet. What happens? Does warm or cold water end up on top? In what way do you think this shows how a front forms when cold and warm air meet in the atmosphere?

MATERIALS

- a small clear plastic or glass container
- modeling clay
- a stiff plastic sheet
- blue food coloring
- 2 mugs
- a spoon
- scissors
- a craft knife
- a steel ruler

WIND DIRECTION

Wind is air moving from one place to another. A wind is described by its direction and strength. We identify the different winds by the direction, or point of the compass, they are blowing from. For example, if the wind is moving from north to south, it is called a northerly. If it is blowing from the east to the west, the wind is called an easterly. We use weather vanes to tell us wind direction. These are turned by the wind to point in the direction the wind is coming from.

Although winds can blow from any direction, most places have a prevailing wind, caused by the global weather pattern. "Prevailing" means the direction from which the wind blows most. Prevailing winds are caused by hot air moving north and south from the equator. The hot air cools as it moves away from the equator toward the poles. Trade winds are prevailing winds at sea. They blow toward the equator from the northeast (Northern Hemisphere) and the southeast (Southern Hemisphere). When ships were powered by sails, the trade winds were very important.

The additional sails, or spinnakers, on these racing yachts enable them to harness more wind power.

A WEATHER VANE

1. Choose an open site for the weather vane. Push the thick dowel into the ground. Tie one 12-in. (30-cm) length of dowel to the thick dowel, about 8 in. (20 cm) below the top, so that the thin dowel is horizontal. Tie the other 12-in. (30-cm) dowel at right angles to the first. Secure with modeling clay.

2. Use a compass to find which direction is north. Turn the thick dowel until one end of one of the thin dowels is pointing north. Cut letters N, S, E, and W from a piece of balsa wood. Paint them and leave to dry. Then tie them firmly to the ends of the thin dowels.

3. Straighten out the paper clip. Tape it to the top of the thick dowel so that it sticks up about 4 in. (10 cm) above the top. Use modeling clay to hold the paper clip in place while you tape it.

4. Now make a pointer. With rubber bands, attach the pen cap to the middle of the 20-in. (50-cm) dowel. When the pen cap is vertical, the dowel should be horizontal. Cut one piece of balsa wood about 2 in. x 4 in. (5 cm x 10 cm), and another to make an arrowhead. Paint both and tie to either end of the dowel.

5. Put the pen cap over the paper clip on the thick dowel. To balance the pointer, stick small coins on the arrowhead with blobs of modeling clay. The pointer will swing to point in the direction the wind is coming from.

29

BREEZES AND GALES

Wind speed is measured in miles per hour, kilometers per hour, or knots (nautical miles per hour). The Beaufort scale rates wind speed from 0 (calm) to 12 (hurricane), but to get an accurate measurement, you need to use an anemometer. Most anemometers have three to four cups attached to a vertical axle. These cups catch the wind. The higher the wind speed, the faster the axle spins. The wind speed is shown on a mechanical or electronic scale.

The wind speed near the ground is always lower than it is higher in the air. That is because hills, trees, and buildings slow the moving air and make the wind more gusty. Wind speed is always higher, and the wind less gusty, on mountaintops and at sea.

The wind has a marked effect on how hot or cold the air feels. Your body warms the air close to it. In the wind, this warm air is blown away and replaced by cooler air, which cools your body. This is called windchill factor. The stronger the wind, the more heat is lost from your body and the colder it feels.

AN ANEMOMETER

1. Straighten a large paper clip and tape it to the top of the dowel so that it sticks up about 4 in. (10 cm) above the top. Choose an open site for your anemometer, away from buildings and trees. Push the dowel firmly into the ground.

2. Cut the top off the plastic bottle. From the remaining plastic, cut two half-cylinder pieces of plastic about 6 in. (15 cm) long.

MATERIALS

- a large plastic bottle
- a 5-ft. (1.5-m) length of dowel
- a pen cap
- a stapler
- large and small paper clips
- modeling clay
- scissors
- a ruler
- tape
- a hole punch

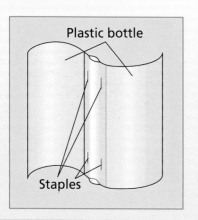

Plastic bottle

Staples

3. Overlap the edges of the two plastic pieces by about 1 in. (3 cm) to make an S shape with a narrow tube up the center. Staple the pieces together, as shown in the diagram, leaving one end of the tube open. Push a pen cap, closed end first, into the open end of the tube.

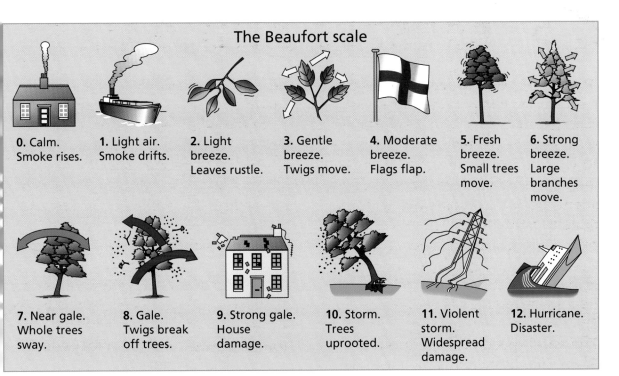

The Beaufort scale

0. Calm. Smoke rises.

1. Light air. Smoke drifts.

2. Light breeze. Leaves rustle.

3. Gentle breeze. Twigs move.

4. Moderate breeze. Flags flap.

5. Fresh breeze. Small trees move.

6. Strong breeze. Large branches move.

7. Near gale. Whole trees sway.

8. Gale. Twigs break off trees.

9. Strong gale. House damage.

10. Storm. Trees uprooted.

11. Violent storm. Widespread damage.

12. Hurricane. Disaster.

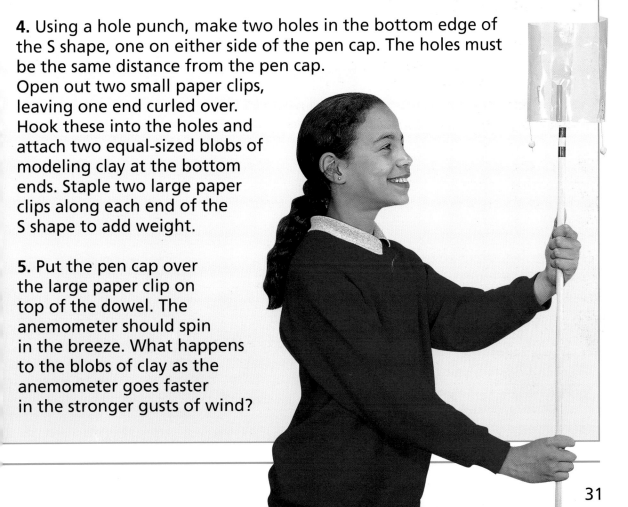

4. Using a hole punch, make two holes in the bottom edge of the S shape, one on either side of the pen cap. The holes must be the same distance from the pen cap.
Open out two small paper clips, leaving one end curled over. Hook these into the holes and attach two equal-sized blobs of modeling clay at the bottom ends. Staple two large paper clips along each end of the S shape to add weight.

5. Put the pen cap over the large paper clip on top of the dowel. The anemometer should spin in the breeze. What happens to the blobs of clay as the anemometer goes faster in the stronger gusts of wind?

CLIMATES

Have you ever traveled to another part of the world where the weather was quite unlike the weather at home? Different places around the world have different patterns of weather throughout the year. Climate is the word for the pattern of weather that it is usual for a place to have.

There are many factors that affect the climate of a place: how near it is to the equator, how near or far it is from the sea, and whether it is in or near mountains. There are nine different types of climate around the world. They are polar, cold forests, temperate, mediterranean, desert, dry grassland, mountain, subtropical, and tropical. In general, it is always hot near the equator, always cold near the poles. Between these two extremes the climate is temperate, and there are four seasons—spring, summer, autumn, and winter. Mountains create their own climates as air flows up and over them. It always gets colder the higher you climb up a mountain.

The desert climate of the Sahara in Africa is hot and dry all year round. The winds that blow across it contain very little moisture.

Even in the harshest climates, animals and plants have adapted to survive. In desert regions, for example, plants store precious water in their fleshy leaves. Many animals, such as jerboas and foxes, spend the day sheltering from the baking heat in underground burrows, where the temperature is several degrees cooler.

DID YOU KNOW?

Quito in Ecuador is said to have the most pleasant climate of any place in the world. It is warm and spring-like all year round, with small, refreshing amounts of rain.

A WORLD CLIMATE MAP

1. Draw a simple world map in the center of the blue poster board, leaving plenty of space around it. Alternatively, trace and cut out the map from green poster board and stick it onto the blue poster board.

2. Search through newspapers, magazines, and travel brochures for color pictures of places around the world that show what the climate is like there. Try to find a picture for each of the climates listed on page 32. Use an atlas to find out where the countries are and tape the photos near them on the blue poster board. Draw a line from each country to its photo. Does your climate map give you a good idea of the way climates change around the world?

3. Look in today's newspaper to find out what the weather is like in the places on your map. Also, look in the atlas at average rainfall and sunshine figures. Does the information you have found match the pictures? If not, can you explain why not?

4. Can you see any examples of people and animals adapting to the climate in the pictures on your map?

MATERIALS

- a large sheet of blue poster board about 16 in. x 24 in. (40 cm x 60 cm)
- a sheet of green poster board
- an atlas
- old newspapers, magazines, and travel brochures
- scissors
- tape or glue
- a pencil
- felt-tip pens

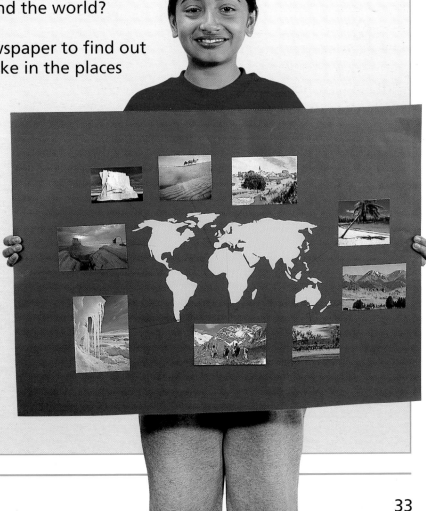

WINTER WEATHER

Areas of the earth that are far from the equator have very cold winters. Low temperatures are accompanied by snow, frost, and fog. There is also wintery weather high up on mountains, even those peaks near the equator. The reason for this is that the average air temperature falls by about 1.8° F (1° C) for every 1,300 ft. (400 m) you go up through the atmosphere.

Inside most clouds, even in the summer, the temperature is very low. Ice crystals in the cloud become larger and collide with each other, to form snowflakes. These fall out of the cloud and, if it is cold enough, reach the ground as snow without melting into rain. Snowflakes usually have six sides. In colder air, they are long and thin, shaped like needles or rods. In slightly warmer air, they form delicate star shapes. But no two snowflakes are ever the same, no matter how many you look at.

Deep snow may look picturesque, but it can be hazardous for people and animals.

ICE TEST

Fill the plastic bottle to the brim and screw the top on tightly. Wrap the bottle in a plastic bag and put it in a freezer. Leave it for a few hours until the water has frozen. What has happened to the bottle? Can you imagine how ice can break up rocks in the same way?

MATERIALS
- a plastic bottle
- a plastic bag

Frost and fog are two common features of winter weather. On clear, cold nights, when the ground cools more quickly than the air, water vapor in the air condenses on the ground, making dew. If the temperature of the air falls below freezing, the water vapor turns into ice crystals, or frost. If warm, very damp air, such as the air over a river or pond, cools at night, water vapor condenses to form fog, which is like a low cloud.

DEW TRAP

MATERIALS
- a plastic bottle
- warm water
- a bowl of cold water

1. Fill the bottle one-quarter full with warm water. Swirl the water around a few times and then pour it out. This leaves you with a warm bottle full of warm air.

2. Plunge the bottom of the bottle into cold water. Can you see condensation forming on the inside of the bottle? This is exactly how dew forms on cold ground after a warm day.

SNOW SHAPES

MATERIALS
- a metal tray
- gloves
- a magnifying glass

When it is snowing outside, put the metal tray in the freezer until it is very cold. Put gloves on and quickly carry the tray outside. Allow some snowflakes to fall onto the tray. Look closely at the flakes with a magnifying glass. Can you see the six-sided shapes? Try making some sketches of them.

THUNDERSTORMS

A huge thunderstorm, with dazzling forks of lightning, is a truly spectacular sight. Thunderstorms occur in warm, humid conditions, when dark, towering cumulonimbus clouds build up in the sky.

Lightning is caused by static electricity. You know how your hair sometimes stands on end when you comb it? That effect is caused by static electricity, too. When two objects rub against each other, static electricity often builds up. One of the objects becomes positively charged and the other becomes negatively charged. The two charges attract each other, which is why your hair is pulled toward your comb. If the charge on an object becomes great enough, it leaps off, creating a spark.

Inside cumulonimbus clouds, the air swirls up and down at high speed. The water droplets and ice crystals are smashed into each other, creating static electricity. Gradually, the top of the cloud becomes positively charged and the bottom becomes negatively charged. Sometimes a spark leaps from one end of the cloud to the other,

Cloud-to-ground lightning strikes from a thundercloud at sunset.

making a bright flash. Sometimes it leaps to the ground, making a fork or zigzag. The spark heats the air around it very quickly. The hot air expands, causing the rumbling noise of thunder.

DID YOU KNOW?

You see lightning before you hear thunder because light travels faster than sound. Sound takes about five seconds to travel one mile (1.6 km). When you see a flash of lightning, start counting the seconds until you hear the thunder. Can you figure out how far away the lightning is from the number of seconds?

MINI-LIGHTNING

1. Press a large blob of modeling clay into the middle of the tray to make a handle. Lay the trash bag on a flat surface. **Do not use a surface that might get scratched.** Have a metal spoon ready. Turn the light out or close the curtains to make the room dark.

2. Rub the tray across the trash bag for about 30 seconds. Don't touch the tray, only the modeling clay.

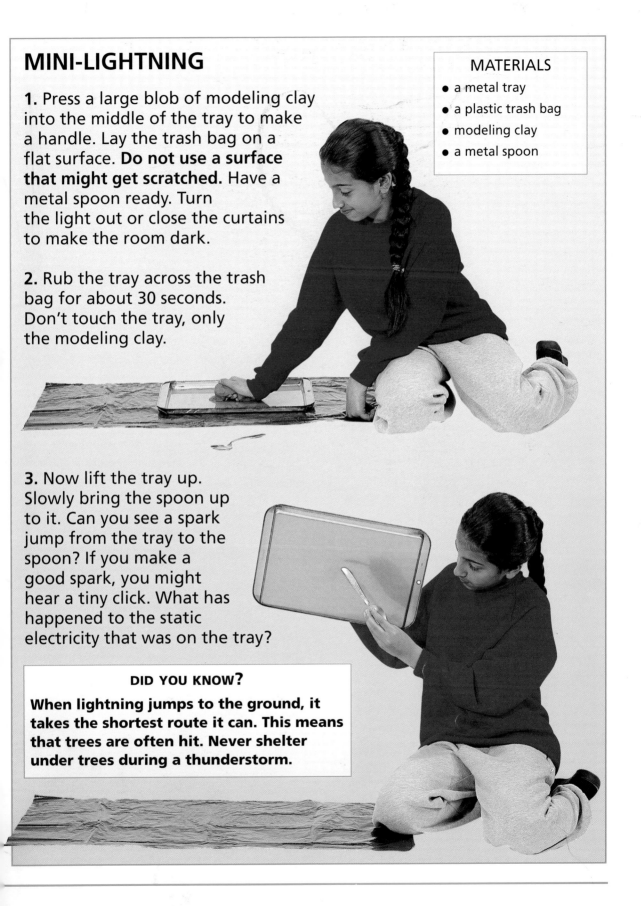

3. Now lift the tray up. Slowly bring the spoon up to it. Can you see a spark jump from the tray to the spoon? If you make a good spark, you might hear a tiny click. What has happened to the static electricity that was on the tray?

DID YOU KNOW?

When lightning jumps to the ground, it takes the shortest route it can. This means that trees are often hit. Never shelter under trees during a thunderstorm.

DANGEROUS WEATHER

The weather is at its most dangerous when it creates very strong winds. In hurricanes (also called cyclones) and tornadoes, winds can blow at more than 180 mph (300 km/h). They are easily capable of uprooting trees, tearing roofs from buildings, and whipping up huge waves at sea.

A hurricane is a depression with very low pressure at the center. As it travels across the warm sea, it gathers energy. The winds circling around it grow stronger and stronger. Once they reach land, the winds begin to die down, but they can still be extremely destructive. Weather forecasters use satellites to keep track of hurricanes so that they can tell when one is going to hit a certain area. This way, they can warn the people living there before the hurricane strikes.

A tornado is a swirling column of air that reaches down from a huge thundercloud. The column is often less than 300 ft. (100 m) across, but the winds inside it are even stronger than those in a hurricane. Animals, people, and even cars can be lifted off the ground by the rapidly spinning air as it

A tornado reaches down from an enormous thundercloud and spirals across the horizon.

passes by. Because the column of air is so narrow, a tornado can destroy one house but leave the house next door untouched.

DID YOU KNOW?

In the center of a hurricane or cyclone is an area of calm a few miles across where the winds are light and the skies are clear. This is called the "eye" of the storm.

A WATER TORNADO

The technical name for the spinning column of air in a tornado is a vortex. Vortexes happen in water, too—you can see one every time you let water flow down the drain in the bathtub. Here's how to make a better version of a water vortex.

1. Cut the top off one of the plastic bottles. This bottle will collect the water from your vortex. Stand it on a firm, level surface.

2. Make a hole in the other bottle top with the hammer and nail.

3. Half-fill this bottle with water and add several drops of food coloring. Put your finger over the hole, turn the bottle upside down, and swirl the water around. When it is moving well, hold the bottle steady and place it over the other bottle. The water should still be swirling.

4. Now remove your finger. Can you see a vortex? The water should form a funnel shape as it flows out, with air moving up the center of the vortex into the bottle. It might take you a few attempts to get the spinning action right.

5. Vortexes can spin clockwise and counterclockwise. Can you make water vortexes that go both ways?

WEATHER RECORDING

The study of weather is called meteorology, and scientists who study the weather are called meteorologists. Recording the weather accurately is very important because it helps meteorologists see weather patterns and make weather forecasts (see page 42). In some parts of the world, weather records go back for hundreds of years. These records show how weather patterns have changed over the centuries.

Weather is recorded at weather stations, where there are measuring instruments, such as thermometers, anemometers,

A SUNSHINE RECORDER

This project will work only when the sun is shining for uninterrupted periods of at least an hour long.

MATERIALS
- a large, clear plastic bottle
- a black plastic trash bag
- 2 pieces of thick cardboard, 8 in. x 12 in. (20 x 30 cm)
- scissors
- tape

1. Fill the bottle with water. Stand it on a piece of cardboard on a firm, level surface where it will be in the sunshine all day.

2. Cut three strips of black trash bag about 12 in. (30 cm) long and 2 in. (5 cm) wide. Attach them to the other piece of cardboard with tape as in the picture.

3. Hold the cardboard close to the bottle, on the opposite side of the sun. Move the cardboard back and forth. At a certain distance from the bottle, the sunlight will be focused into a narrow strip. Bend the cardboard into a semicircle so that all parts of it are the same distance from the bottle. Attach it to the cardboard base with tape.

4. As the day goes by, and the sun moves across the sky, the strip of light will move around the semicircle. When the sun is shining brightly, the heat rays will make the plastic shrink. This automatically records when the sun is in or out.

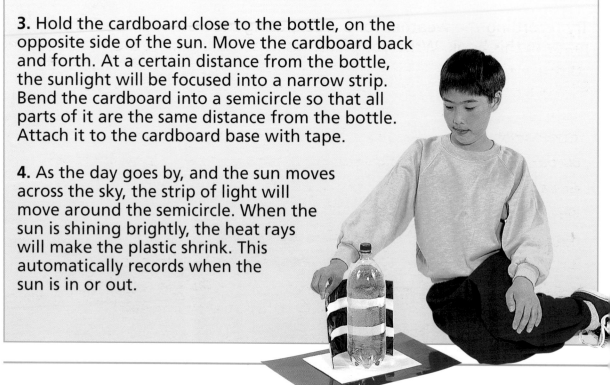

barometers, hygrometers, rain gauges, and sunshine recorders. Some instruments have built-in clocks and record on a strip of paper how readings change hour by hour.

At some weather stations, a meteorologist has to read all the instruments at the same time each day and write down the readings. Other weather stations are completely automatic; they send their readings to a meteorological center by telephone or radio.

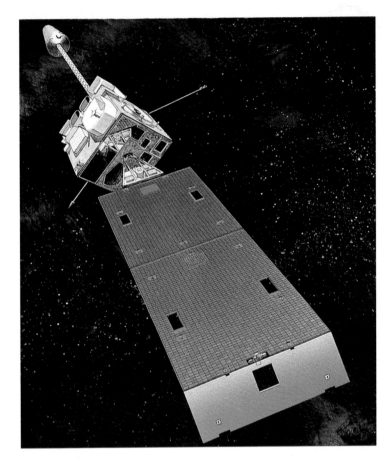

Meteorologists use satellites such as this to help with their weather predictions.

RECORDING THE WEATHER

Try recording the weather for a week, using the instruments you have made in this book. Write your findings in a notebook. At the end of the week, can you determine the average temperature and rainfall per day? Below is a list of instruments and the types of readings they give.

Thermometer	— shows temperature in degrees F or C
Barometer	— tells you if atmospheric pressure is rising or falling
Anemometer	— tells you wind speed (light, medium, or strong)
Weather vane	— shows wind direction
Hygrometer	— tells you if it is damp or dry
Rain gauge	— shows the amount of rain in inches or mm
Sunshine recorder	— shows the amount of sunshine. (You have to estimate the percentage each day was sunny.)

WEATHER FORECASTING

Accurate forecasts make harvesting easier to plan.

Knowing what the weather will be like in advance is useful if you are planning a day out or trying to decide what clothes to wear. For some people, however, weather predictions are absolutely vital. Sailors and pilots use weather forecasts to plan their routes so that they can take advantage of the wind or avoid bad weather.

YOUR OWN FORECAST

1. Make a map of the part of the country where you live by cutting it out of colored cardboard. Copy it from a newspaper weather map. If you live on the coast make the land green and the sea blue. Glue the map onto the large sheet of white cardboard and pin it to a bulletin board.

2. Make weather symbols to stick on the map. You can get ideas for these from newspaper and television forecasts. Make the shapes out of colored cardboard. Press putty onto the backs to hold them on the map.

3. Look in a newspaper for a weather forecast for today and tomorrow. From the information, plan your own television-style, 30-second weather forecast to present to your friends or family. Write down what you are going to say (this is called a script) and plan which weather symbols to put on your map. Practice a few times before you do it for your friends.

MATERIALS

- a large sheet of white cardboard about 16 x 24 in. (40 x 60 cm)
- sheets of thin cardboard in assorted colors
- putty
- scissors and glue
- a newspaper weather map
- a bulletin board
- thumbtacks

Farmers consult long-term forecasts to find the best times for planting crops and harvesting.

Most countries have their own meteorological services, which collect and records weather readings and use these to forecast the weather. Newspaper and television forecasters get their information from this service.

Forecasting the weather is a difficult job. In the past, people used their experiences of watching the weather to determine what it might do; but this only gave them forecasts for up to several hours ahead. Today, weather forecasts are worked out by powerful computers. Information from weather stations and weather balloons is fed into a computer, which analyzes it and calculates how conditions might look over the next few hours or days.

Forecasters also use weather satellites and radar. Satellites send back pictures of clouds, which show up how depressions and fronts are moving. Radar can detect rainfall over very wide areas. Radar is often so accurate that it can forecast rain almost to the minute.

> **DID YOU KNOW?**
>
> **Television weather forecasters do not stand in front of a real map; they stand in front of a blue screen. The map is created by a computer. Studio technicians superimpose an image of the map onto the screen by electronic means.**

4. How did your presentation go? Did it last exactly 30 seconds? You could ask somebody to videotape your forecast so that you can see it yourself on television—and correct your mistakes!

ATMOSPHERIC POLLUTION

Pollution comes in many forms, from chemicals poured into rivers to litter thrown onto the streets. One kind of pollution that is not so obvious is atmospheric pollution. This is caused by the gases produced by burning fuels in power stations, factories, homes, vehicles, and aircraft. Different waste gases have different polluting effects.

The effects of atmospheric pollution can be catastrophic. Exposure to acid rain has devastated this forest of spruce trees in Poland.

THE GREENHOUSE EFFECT

1. Remove or cut the lid off the cardboard box. Cover the box with the clear plastic sheet or plastic wrap, holding it in place with tape. Pierce a small hole for the thermometer in the side of the box.

MATERIALS
- a large cardboard box
- clear plastic sheet or plastic wrap
- a thermometer
- tape
- scissors

2. Leave the box in the sunshine for a few minutes. Measure the temperature in a shaded area outside the box and then inside the box (making sure the thermometer bulb stays in the shade). Is the temperature different? Can you explain why?

One of the most striking effects of pollution is smog. If high pressure settles over a built-up area, still conditions are created and smog occurs. Exhaust gases from vehicles build, and the air becomes hazy with a thin, yellowish fog. Some people find it hard to breathe in bad smog.

The term "global warming" refers to the fact that the world's weather seems to be getting gradually warmer, and climates seem to be changing.

The warming may be caused by the greenhouse effect, which traps the sun's heat in the atmosphere. Polluting gases and deforestation (the cutting down of the world's forests) are major causes of an increased greenhouse effect. Sulfur dioxide gas (and some other types of gas) combines with water droplets in the air, turning the water into acid. This falls as acid rain, which eats away buildings and kills trees and water-living animals.

AN ACID RAIN TEST

1. Tear a few cabbage leaves into small pieces and put them in the bowl. Ask an adult to help you pour some boiling water from the tea kettle into the bowl. Mash the leaves with a wooden spoon for a few minutes and then leave the water to cool. The water will turn blue.

2. Strain the cabbage leaves and pour the cooled cabbage water into the first glass jar. Throw away the leaves. Next time it rains, collect some rainwater in the second jar (or from your rain gauge). Put some tap water into the third jar. Label each jar.

3. Pour some cabbage water into each jar. Is there any difference in color between the jars?

MATERIALS

- a red cabbage
- a wooden spoon
- 3 small glass jars
- a bowl
- a tea kettle of boiling water
- a strainer or colander
- self-stick labels and felt-tip pens

WARNING!

- Be careful when using the tea kettle.

GLOSSARY

Air pressure The push exerted by air because of the movement of its molecules.

Anemometer A device for measuring the speed of the wind.

Anticyclone Any region in the atmosphere where the air pressure is increased.

Atmosphere The thick blanket of air that surrounds the earth.

Atmospheric pressure The air pressure in the atmosphere. It is normally measured at sea level.

Barometer A device for measuring air pressure.

Climate The pattern of weather that a place on Earth experiences.

Concentric circles Two or more circles of different sizes, but with the same point as their centers.

Condensation The process that takes place when water vapor cools and turns into liquid water.

Cyclone The word for a hurricane in the Southern Hemisphere.

Density The mass of a certain volume of a material.

Depression A region in the atmosphere where the air pressure is reduced.

Evaporation The process that takes place when liquid water turns into water vapor. Evaporation takes place when water boils, but it can also happen at a temperature below boiling point.

Front A junction between a mass of warm air and a mass of cool air.

High Another name for an anticyclone.

Humidity A measure of the amount of water vapor in the air.

Hurricane A depression with very low pressure and high winds.

Hygrometer A device for measuring humidity.

Low Another name for a depression.

Radar A device that detects objects in the air by sending out radio waves and receiving any that bounce back.

Thermal A rising current of warm air.

Thermometer A device for measuring temperature.

Vortex A swirling column of air or water.

Water vapor The gaseous form of water.

Weather vane A device for measuring the direction of the wind.

FURTHER INFORMATION

BOOKS

Ardley, Neil. *The Science Book of Weather.* San Diego: Harcourt Brace, 1992.

Bramwell, Martyn. *Weather* (Earth Science Library). Danbury, CT: Franklin Watts, 1994.

Cosgrove, Brian. *Weather* (Eyewitness Guides). New York: Knopf Books for Young Readers, 1991.

Ganeri, Anita. *Weather* (Nature Detective). Danbury, CT: Franklin Watts, 1993.

Gardner, Robert and David Webster. *Science Projects About Weather* (Science Projects). Springfield, NJ: Enslow Publishers, 1994.

Simon, Seymour. *Weather.* New York: Morrow Junior Books, 1993.

CD-ROMS

Exploring Land Habitats. Raintree Steck-Vaughn, 1997.

Exploring Water Habitats. Raintree Steck-Vaughn, 1997.

ANSWERS TO QUESTIONS

Answers to questions posed in the projects.

Pages 4–5 Air Has Weight: Air escapes from the punctured balloon, making it lighter. Under Pressure: Sucking air from the bottle reduces the pressure inside. The higher air pressure outside the bottle presses the sides inward.

Pages 8–9 The black cardboard is best at absorbing the sun's heat. When the sun is high in the sky, it heats the ground more than when it is low in the sky.

Pages 10–11 With the globe leaning away from the flashlight, the Southern Hemisphere receives the most sunshine. It is winter in the Northern Hemisphere.

Pages 12–13 Balloon Tricks: The air in the balloon contracts when it cools, and the air in the bottle expands when it warms up. Air Spinner: Air warmed by the warm water rises through the propeller, making it spin.

Pages 14–15 In the sunshine, the sun's rays heat the thermometer. The foil protects the thermometer from the sun's rays and the open tube allows air to circulate.

Pages 16–17 Evaporation: The uncovered dish dries out first because the air can carry away the water vapor above it.

Paper Strip Hygrometer: The paper strip stretches slightly when it gets damp and contracts as it dries out.

Pages 18–19 A Cloud Maker: Water vapor in the warm air above the water mixes with cold air under the ice and condenses into tiny drops.

Pages 26–27 The warm water rises over the cold water just as warm air rises over cold air at a weather front.

Pages 30–31 As the wind strength increases, the anemometer spins faster, pushing the blobs of clay farther out and up.

Pages 34–35 Ice Test: Water seeps into narrow cracks in rocks. If it freezes, it expands and can widen the cracks.

Pages 36–37 The charge of static electricity on the tray has jumped to the ground, making the tray neutral again.

Pages 44–45 The Greenhouse Effect: The temperature in the box rises because the heat that enters through the plastic wrap cannot escape through it. An Acid Rain Test: If the rainwater turns red, it means that the rain is slightly acidic.

INDEX